From the CoolREADS series…

Why Retirement Sucks (for Some of Us, Anyway) and What to do About It

A Handbook for Life After Your Day Job Goes Away

D1293207

By Jim Schell

Co-Author of Small Business for Dummies

For distribution information please call:

Lights On Publishing
541-788-7137
Bend, Oregon

Printed in the United States of America

Contents

Why I am Qualified to Write This CoolREADS

I'm a recovering entrepreneur; I haven't had a business to run for 27 years. No people responsibilities, no office hours, and nary a paycheck to sign since 1990. So, what do you think, does that make me retired?

Stumped? Allow me to answer my own question: Whether or not I'm retired depends on your definition of the word "retired." If retired means I no longer have a payroll to meet, then yes, I'm retired. If retired means I can sleep in following a rare late night out, then yes, I'm retired. If retired means that Mary (my wife) and I can head for the golf course on a moment's notice, then yes, I'm retired.

If, on the other hand, retired means that I no longer have any meaningful ventures to pursue, then no, I'm not retired. If retired means that I no longer have any young people to teach, mentor, and train, then no, I'm not retired. If retired means that I'm not making a positive difference in my community, then no, I'm not retired.

In essence then, notwithstanding the fact that the federal government began sending me Social Security checks 18 years ago, I do not consider myself to be retired. The reason? How can any dedicated ex-entrepreneur (or ex-anything, for that matter) pack up a career of passion and commitment and walk away from it? After all, I spent my working life being driven to make a difference in the lives of my employees, my customers, and those who believed in me. As a result, I've learned that it's impossible to select a random date on the calendar and determine that, after that date has passed, I will no longer be driven. Sorry, but my adrenaline needs a reason to run.

Oh, I tried to retire. It was a month-long exercise of frustration. I worked harder at trying to make retirement work than I ever did at making my careers work. The need to work came easy to me—my parents saw to that. They both grew up on small farms in Iowa. Farm life means that you learn early on what work is all about and then, if you're like my parents, you pass that ethic on to your kids. This is what happened to me, which means my mom and dad are to blame for my love of work.

While I failed miserably at retiring, I haven't failed at the whatever-you-want-to-call-it part of life that comes after one's primary career is over. Since the end of my first career as an entrepreneur, I've added three more careers to the list. They include writing six published books (not counting the six CoolREADS I've recently written), founding five nonprofits and leading three nonprofit turnarounds, and, just now, at the ripe young age of 80, a cooler-than-cool for-profit business (presently sans paycheck), the very same company that published this book. I've also served on a half-dozen boards in the last several years, mentored several hundred young men and women (yes, several hundred) over the last 27 years, and found time to travel with Mary and play my fair share of golf.

In his book *The Retiring Mind: How to Make the Psychological Transition to Retirement,* Robert Delamontagne makes the point that the more you are defined by the work you do, the harder it will be to make the transition to retirement. He goes on to say that people who have an achievement addiction as a result of their work life are the same folks who have the most difficulty transitioning into retirement.

I'm mostly guilty as charged. But, I should add, I'm okay with that guilt, and I wouldn't have it any other way. I don't see myself as being defined by my work, although I loved most of what I did over a 25-year entrepreneurial career. I am, however, addicted to the feeling of achievement that comes with doing whatever it is I set out to do or, in some cases, with simply doing what entrepreneurs are bred to do—get shit done. That's because getting shit done is what I do best and when I'm finished getting it done, I start looking for more of it to do. So yes, I'm an achievement addict, and I'm happy to say that my addiction is currently going untreated. I hope that will never change.

Introduction

"The greatest potential for growth and self-realization exists in the second half of life." – **Carl Jung**

In April 2006, a story from the *LA Times* became one of national interest. It involved Arthur Winston, a longtime employee of the Los Angeles Metropolitan Transportation Authority (MTA). Mr. Winston worked for the MTA for over 72 years, missing only one day of work. Why that one day? He took it off to attend his wife's funeral in 1988. Known as "Mr. Reliable," Arthur Winston, son of an Oklahoma cotton picker, received an "Employee of the Century" citation from President Bill Clinton.

On his 100th birthday, less than one month after retiring, Arthur Winston died in his sleep. Old age—or so the newswires said, anyway—had finally caught up with him.

"Horsefeathers" is all I have to say to that. What really caught up with Arthur Winston was the fact that his need to work was no longer being satisfied. Like broadcast journalists Andy Rooney and Morley Safer, Arthur NEEDED to work.

I'm not implying that retirement is going to "catch up" with everyone who elects to opt for it. A recent Mass Mutual study tells us that 72% of our nation's retirees report being "extremely or quite happy" doing what they're doing. More power to that 72%, I would say; if you're one of them I wish you a long and happy life. And then, in the next breath, I'd advise you that reading this CoolREADS is going to be a waste of your time, as it is written for the other 28%. Incidentally, that 28% represents about 90 million Americans, so that's a good number of folks who are candidates for reading this book.

This CoolREADS is not about retiring. Rather, it's about what our un-retirement options will be when it comes time to make the decision to retire. Thanks to my inherited need to work and 27 years of experience at un-retiring, I'm a self-appointed expert on the topic.

So, how do you know if you're one of the 28%? If any one of the following statements applies to you, you're a solid candidate:

> 1) Work may be a four-letter word in the dictionary but it's a three-letter word to you. Those three letters spell "fun," and you love to have it. Or at least, you have fun when the work you're doing is something enjoyable and meaningful. The trick, then, is to find something to do in this un-retirement stage that provides joy and a sense of purpose. Don't worry, there are plenty of options out there (see chapters

seven and eight for some of them).

2) Making a difference in other people's lives has always been appealing to you. In your pre-retirement days, you found that helping other people usually benefits you as much as it does them. You may have helped other people who worked with or for you. You may have volunteered for organizations that did cool stuff for people. Or you may just be one of those folks who look for little old ladies to help cross the street. In any event, helping others feels good when you do it.

3) Mental stimulation is important to you. You've tried crossword puzzles, Words with Friends, and Sudoku. They were fun but soon ran their course. You need something more stimulating to commit your time to.

4) The world you live in has been good to you, and you'd like to give something back. To get this far in life you've used those institutions, organizations, and assets in your community that others have built: schools, parks, nonprofits, etc. It's now time to do some building of your own.

5) You're addicted to achievement and, yes, to getting shit done. Once you've been in that zone, it's hard to walk away.

Do you see yourself in at least one of these statements? If you do, you may be one of the 90 million of us for whom a traditional retirement isn't going to work. Sure, we non-retirees may be in the minority where the United States is concerned, but in our community there are still plenty of us to go around, which means you'll be hanging out with like-minded people. Things could be a lot worse than spending time with people who are addicted to achievement.

This CoolREADS is for those 90 million Americans who are at or above retirement age (62 according to Social Security, 55 according to the state I live in) and who do not fall into the "extremely or quite happy" category. It is also for the millions of baby boomers who are approaching the age of retirement and are wondering whether or not it's going to work for them. My goal with this CoolREADS is to help those of you who have the potential to be part of the 90 million of us who are looking for a solution to the post-retirement phase of our life.

Chapter One

Looking Down on Retirement from Above

"To retire is the beginning of death." – **Pablo Casals, one of the greatest cellists of all time**

"Hmm, I think you're overstating the case against retirement," I would say to Pablo if he were still among us. If he had added the suffix "for me" to the end of his sentence, *then* I'd be inclined to agree. I have no doubt that had he been deprived of playing the cello for throngs of admiring and cheering audiences over the 30-some years he played beyond retirement age, he would have cashed it all in long before his date with destiny arrived at the ripe age of 97.

I would further tell Pablo I have plenty of friends who are making the most of their retirement years and who enjoy it a heck of a lot more than they enjoyed whatever it was they did in their working years. They are happily going about their retirement gigs: sleeping in, playing golf whenever they feel like it, and visiting their grandkids on a whim. Such activities may not have worked for people like Pablo, but they work just fine for many of my friends, along with millions of other Americans.

Those retirement-enjoying friends of mine are upstanding people, I should add. They're also friends in the true sense of the word. I see them frequently, play golf with them often, and occasionally bend elbows with them over a beer or coffee. Besides, the world would not be a better place if everyone were like me—or them. In retirement, as in just about everything else, diversity is key.

Before you read any further, I should warn you that there are dozens, if not hundreds, of books written on the topic of retirement. This is not one of them. There are very few books written on the topic of un-retirement. This *is* one of them.

But before we go any further, let's define some words we'll be using in this CoolREADS. Here are four definitions you'll need to know:

> **Retirement:** Webster's definition is *"withdrawal from one's position or occupation or from active working life."*

> **Retired:** By extension of Webster's definition then, a person who is "retired" is *"someone who has withdrawn from active working life."*

> **Un-Retirement:** Webster avoids defining this word, so I've stepped in. My definition is *"making the choice to continue actively working beyond the age of retirement."*

Un-Retired: Again, by extension, a person who is un-retired is *"someone who has chosen to continue working beyond the age of retirement."*

For four years back in the early 2000s, I served on the Oregon governor's small-business council. Once a month my trusty Jeep and I would make the always-beautiful and sometimes-dicey drive over the Cascade Mountains to Salem, our state capital. There, along with a small group of other business people from around the state, we would spend the day discussing ideas on how our state government could better serve our small-business sector.

Those years were the first time I had the occasion to actually work with public employees, and it proved to be an eye-opening experience in several different ways. One way in particular stands out: the role of retirement as seen through a public employee's eyes. Every employee had a fixed date upon which he was scheduled to retire, a number that was (as I recall) 30 years from the date of his initial employment. Inquire about his retirement date and he would, without a moment of hesitation, inform you that he had five years and 127 days left until the magic date. Then, glancing at his watch, he'd conclude with a smile, "and three hours and 14 minutes."

Contrast his fixed-date answer with that of someone from my small-business/entrepreneurial background: We'd cock our head and look at the questioner like she had just asked us for the square root of 9,873,614. "I dunno," would be our shrugging response, because we wouldn't have the foggiest idea of when we were going to retire. If our business was cooking we'd want to stick with it forever. If our business was struggling, we'd retire in the time it would take to lock the door. Or so we thought, anyway. In reality, we were too busy fretting about meeting our next payroll to worry about such topics as exit strategy and retirement.

The hallowed rite of retirement in the United States is in turmoil today. The combination of the death of pensions (in the private sector) and our aging population has created, in an unintended consequence sort of way, a change in the way our work lives progress. People are now working longer, a topic we'll discuss at some length in the following chapter. This is a necessary trend for our nation. No longer can we afford to have so many people in their 50s and early 60s exiting the work force so early.

A 2014 Gallup poll determined that the top financial worry for most Americans is "can they afford retirement?" If such a worry is the case, then I have a not-so-earth-shattering idea for those who are worried: don't retire. Or at least postpone your retirement until you can stop worrying about your finances.

So there you have it, my obviously biased, short and sweet words on the topic of retirement, spoken by a guy who unsuccessfully tried it for three weeks before moving on to the next phase of life.

Chapter Two

The System is Broken

"When you're finished changing, you're finished." – **Ben Franklin**

Ben Franklin must have been thinking of our Social Security system when he made the "done changing" statement referenced above. He must have somehow sensed that our venerable retirement system would steadfastly resist change for decades, despite the fact that the people it serves, and the environment within which they are served, have changed so much.

So, how did our nation's Social Security system get so far out of whack? People started living longer—that's the root of the problem.

The Social Security Act was passed way back in 1935, guaranteeing retirement pensions to all Americans at age 62. Those numbers made sense back then, when the life span of an average American was 61. Using the aforementioned numbers and the typical life span back then, our retirees rarely collected more than they had paid into the program, a fact which has played a major role in the system surviving for all these years.

Today, however, an American's average life span hovers somewhere around 80, depending upon whether you're a man (78 years) or a woman (81 years). Thanks to a number of contributing factors, that number will continue to rise for the foreseeable future. What this means is that today's average American can expect to snack at Social Security's shrinking trough for 25 years or more. For me, at my ripe old age of 80, statistics say that I can now expect to celebrate my 90th birthday, which means I'll have been supported by the system for 28 years if I do, in fact, reach that age. For some Americans, these out-of-kilter numbers offer them an opportunity to earn more money from the Social Security system than they did from their work.

In my home state of Oregon, if you're a public employee—state, city, county governments, teachers, etc.—you can retire at age 55 and begin receiving a handsome pension from the State. Kick in Social Security at age 62 and it's no wonder public employees are so focused on their retirement date.

So much has changed over the years. My father worked one job his entire life; 30 years of toiling faithfully (and happily) for the same employer. As a reward for his loyalty, he earned a comfortable pension from his employer when he retired. Meanwhile, those entering today's workforce can expect to have, on average, 11 jobs over the course of their working life. Sorry, kids, but there will be no employer pensions for those of you who choose the private sector. That's one of the prices you pay for the freedom of bouncing around from job to job. My father passed away at age 64, standing in the buffet line at a golf course, after enjoying less than four years of his company's pension and two years of the federal government's. He was a good investment for both of them.

Social Security's underlying assumption back in 1935 was that people aged 60 and higher were in their unproductive years, the years that should be spent on the golf course or in a fishing boat. That assumption is no longer true. My most productive decade was by far my 60s, with my 70s not that far behind. I accomplished more (for our family and for my community) in that decade than any other. I'm a year into my 80s now, and I'm still trying hard to pull my weight. What's happening is that, as a bona fide grizzled veteran, my prolonged years of experience are kicking in. Small wonder that my 60s were my best decade; I had so many more experiences to learn from and lessons to share.

The idea that millions of Americans choose to retire at age earlier rather than later—when most have their productive years still ahead of them—is, at the very least, troubling and, at the very most, frightening. Our governments (both state and federal) can ill afford to offer 30 years of retirement to people in exchange for a matching 30 years of work. The numbers just don't compute, which means, as usual, that the problem will be passed on to our children and grandchildren to resolve.

There's a resolution to the Social Security problem that's been brewing for a dozen years or so. Unfortunately, it hasn't been brewing as quickly as needed, and the federal government hasn't helped matters by continuing to drag their collective feet. But…a partial solution is on the way. Stay tuned for chapter four.

Now that we've identified the reason that the present retirement fiasco isn't working for either our federal government or our 50 states, let's talk about why it also doesn't work for you. Assuming, of course, that you're one of the 90 million people who have a burning need to make shit happen in the upcoming, post-day-job phase of your life.

Chapter Three

Why Retirement Sucks
(for Some of Us, Anyway)

"Retirement kills more people than hard work ever did."

— Malcolm Forbes

Jimmy Carter "retired" from the presidency in 1980. While his presidency failed to garner high grades from those who rate such things, to those of us who have, in our post-career years, strived to make a difference, Jimmy Carter is an out-and-out hero. He's our poster senior.

Carter chose to reinvent himself after losing the 1980 presidential election. He eschewed his political career and instead became a freelance global mediator, statesman, and worldwide health advocate. In forming the Carter Center, he officially hung out his shingle and became a servant of the world, not just the United States. He was 56 when he lost the election and, as this is written, he is 93 and, despite fighting cancer, continues to spend his time doing good work for the world.

"My life since the White House has been more gratifying than before it," Jimmy is quick to say, proving once more that the greatest opportunities can come following a working career, not during it. There are hundreds of thousands, if not millions, of people around the world who have benefited from President Carter's choice to change his career and reinvent himself. Had he chosen to retire and collect speaking fees, he would have been a richer man, but the world would have been poorer. Carter's career should be a lesson for all of us.

Like his our life can become more gratifying as we age.

It would be interesting to hear what went through President Carter's mind when he made the choice to actively pursue a new career. In lieu of seeking his feedback, I've inventoried my own reasons for choosing to shun retirement and start a new career instead. See how many of these reasons apply to you:

1) I'm not comfortable being just another face in the crowd. Unfortunately, I don't have the experience, aptitude, or appetite to play a role in the national or global scene like President Carter, but I am capable of making a difference in my community.

2) I want to wake up each morning excited about life and explore every possibility that comes my way.

3) OK, I'll admit it, I need to work. I can't help it; I'm only doing what I was born to do. (Thanks mom and dad.)

4) I'd miss the adrenaline rush that comes from taking a risk and then watching the venture work. Sure, all ventures aren't going to succeed, but when one does, yesterday's losses are soon forgotten.

5) I need to keep my mind active. Besides enjoying keeping my brain engaged, there is a compelling health reason behind this active-mind choice. Studies conclusively show that Alzheimer's can be slowed or even prevented by keeping the mind active, busy, and at work. (This reason alone would be enough for me!)

The fact that I choose to shun retirement has nothing to do with someone else's decision to retire at age 55 being right or wrong. The two of us simply have different priorities in life. After all, I have a number of good friends who can find plenty of worthwhile ways to pass the time without having to chase yet another career. There is no right or wrong when making the decision of whether or not to retire.

It's often been said that people who choose not to retire do so because they fear the loss of identity that comes from retirement. I'll kind of, sort of agree with that statement, especially when a person is proud of his or her work identity. Even today, as I dive into my 80s, I still want folks to think of me as "the guy who gets shit done." I fear the loss of having a purpose in life, and I fear not having a meaningful mission to pursue.

Even if retirement, in your mind, doesn't suck, and even if you have, over the course of your career, longingly aspired to do it, there's one more reason why retirement may not work for you: You can't afford it.

Here are some sobering statistics that give credence to this statement:

- 36% of Americans have less than $1,000 in their savings account and/or 401(k).
- 60% have under $25,000 in savings.
- 58% have self-admitted "debt problems."
- The median retirement savings for someone in the 55-64 age bracket is $14,500.

And yet, we're told that in order for us to retire and maintain our current standard of living, we need to save somewhere between 10 and 20 times what our annual earnings are. In other words, if we currently bring home $50,000 per year, we need between $500,000 and $1,000,000 in savings to maintain our quality of life.

With these sobering facts in mind, the average American's chances of successfully retiring before, say, age 65 or 70 are slim to none (unless, of course, he or she works for a government or public institution). All of this leads to one inescapable fact: Whether or not most American's think that retirement does in fact suck, they are going to be postponing it for longer than they had previously planned.

With this looming postponement in mind, my recommendation to Mr. Average Working American would be: Shift your dream of retiring at age 55 or 60 towards something more achievable, to something that fits not only your financial situation but also your lifestyle expectations. If you are going to have to spend more years actively involved in a working environment, look for ways to make your new work experiences positive.

Now, let's put a name to what happens once our day job has gone away and we're looking to start a new career. Let's call that new phase of life—drum roll please—an Encore Career.

Chapter Four

Filling the Gap with an Encore Career

"The happiest people I know are the ones who are working. The saddest are the ones who are retired." – **George Burns**

As discussed earlier, our Social Security system has it all wrong. To our federal and state governments and to those keepers of the keys who oversee our Social Security system, I would point out that when the system was devised, our lives consisted of three stages: (1) we grew up (childhood), (2) we had a career (adulthood), and (3) we retired (old age). Those stages have not changed, despite the fact that the model used to devise the system was based on Americans' way of life when the Social Security Act was passed way back in 1935.

Today, four stages need to replace the previous three, with the new, revised model looking something like this: (1) we grow up (childhood), (2) we have a career or careers (adulthood), (3) we have an encore career (encore-hood?), and (4) we retire (old age). Thanks to our lifespan increasing from 61 to 80, the original Social Security model that doesn't include an encore or gap career just doesn't work anymore. It isn't financially sustainable for our governments and it isn't in the best interests of our citizens.

The idea that our prime working years are over at age 60 (or before) is outdated. 60 is the new 50, or so we're told. (It might even be that 60 is the new 45 at the rate things are going.) In fact, our 60s can be even more productive than our previous decades if the kind of work we're doing is right for us.

Now, I must assign credit where credit is due: Thanks to Marc Freedman and his Encore.org organization for introducing the term "encore career" to the English lexicon, as it applies to identifying the gap period between our working career and retirement. Marc and his organization not only coined the term, they have also been responsible for introducing and fostering the encore career movement, designed not only to help our governments balance their budgets but also to keep our senior citizens vibrant and active.

I know firsthand what Marc is talking about. As mentioned earlier, my 60s decade was assuredly the most productive decade of my life, and my 70s were not that far behind. This capability to increase our contribution to society as we age should not be surprising. While we lose a few brain cells as we age, that loss is more than offset by the lessons we've learned thanks to a lifetime of experiences. Those lessons morph into wisdom and, as we old-timers have learned so many times over the years, wisdom trumps brain cells every time.

Is it a national disaster that today's boomers are being forced to work longer than their parents? I don't think so. Rather, I think it's Lifestyle Evolution 101: Since our lives are now spread out over 80 years instead of 60, this stretching out of our working career is the natural consequence. Sooner or later it had to happen. The boomers just happen to be the generation backed into making the transition. Yes, they're feeling the pain, but they're also leading the way. Someone has to be the pioneer.

I view this forced transition as a national opportunity that will lead to expanding our workforce, boosting our economy, and helping our senior population age gracefully. Today's boomers are the disrupters of our nation's traditional working environment—tomorrow they'll be our heroes.

Chapter Five

The Need to Live, Love, Learn, and Leave a Legacy

"Retirement is the ugliest word in the English language."
— Ernest Hemingway

I enjoy fixing things, and I'm good at it. No, I'm not talking about repairing leaky faucets or broken light switches, I'm talking about fixing broken organizations, especially for-profit businesses and nonprofit agencies. Over the years I've "fixed" a number of organizations in my community, a process that is generally stressful and not a lot of fun but, when finished, can be extremely rewarding.

It was sometime in the early 2000s, I was in my Mr. Fixit mode and working with our local Humane Society, a broken organization in need of a shake-up. It was stressful work. The executive director needed to be replaced, staff needed to be upgraded, and old board members needed to be succeeded by new ones. Oddly enough, I enjoy the roller coaster of emotions that evolves from doing this kind of a project. The highs that come at the end always outweigh the lows that take place at the beginning.

In the middle of that muddle someone recommended that I read Dr. Stephen Covey's book, *The Seven Habits of Highly Effective People*. In the course of reading it, I came across a section in the book that answered questions I had been asking myself for the preceding half-dozen years: "Why do I continue to do all the volunteer stuff, especially when it involves so much stress and conflict, when I could be on a golf course with other people my age? What's the pull? What's in this for me?"

Mary also asked me these types of questions whenever I'd trudge home at night and complain about the stress and conflict of the current situation. My typical answer was usually a shrug, followed by something along the lines of "I like giving back." Deep down, I had always suspected there was something more personal going on. I just wasn't sure what that "something more" was. Yes, I knew I needed to stay busy, and I needed to be working on something meaningful, but the overriding questions still lingered, and the answer hadn't come.

Until, that is, I read Dr. Covey's book. In it, he informs us that in order for a person to be happy, the four "Ls" must be present in life:

1. **Live:** We need a roof over our head and a fridge filled with food.
2. **Love:** We need someone or something to love.

3. **Learn:** We need to be constantly learning.
4. **Leave a Legacy:** We need to always be working on leaving a legacy.

The first two of the four Ls, live and love, were alive and well in my life. Mary and I had a roof over our heads, and we knew where our next meals were coming from. In fulfilling Covey's love requirement, I had married far over my head—a feat that made every day a good one.

The most elusive of Covey's four Ls for me was the fourth one: leaving a legacy. This L requires that you pursue a meaningful goal that makes a difference. That pursuit could include joining, fixing, or starting a nonprofit organization; mentoring, coaching, or teaching the next generation; and/or helping a for-profit business grow and succeed. It could be helping people turn their lives around or creating something that enhances your community. There is no shortage of legacy opportunities in your neighborhood.

Sorry, but yesterday's already-achieved legacies don't count. Sure, your kids may have been your legacy, but they're grown and flown. If they're anything like mine, they have their own lives and are no longer within your sphere of influence. Yes, your working career may have been your legacy, but those days have passed, and your previous career has been handed over to someone new. The legacy you adopt must be a new one, a fresh one, something that is meaningful to the rest of the world and especially to you.

What's considered a legacy is in the eye of the beholder. For me, a legacy is something that benefits society and will outlive me. Others may have a different definition. I know people who see their grandchildren as their legacy. For some, restoring an old car may be a legacy, for others, creating something of value with their bare hands might fill the bill.

No matter how one defines the word legacy, in Covey's mind (and in mine), the pursuit of it must never end. Once you've concluded the legacy you're working on, you'll need to find another to take its place. You may not ever conclude your legacy, Covey says, but you'll always need to have one in progress.

Not far behind leaving a legacy in order of importance is the third L, learning. The older you get the more you realize how little you know and how many unfilled gaps there are in your knowledge base. The act of filling those gaps at an advanced age is not only energizing, it plays an important role in warding off the aging blues. How many times have you met someone who, at your age or older, has decided to go back to school, or start a new job, or learn a new skill? Your reaction to that person is usually some form of awe mixed with respect, awe that this person would choose to spend time and energy adding a new dimension to his or her life, and respect that he or she would set out to learn something new at a time when most people are on cruise control.

With apologies to the departed master, I would add a qualifier to Dr. Covey's "Everyone, to be happy..." sentence. I would change that sentence to read: "Everyone, to be **truly** happy, must have the four Ls in his or her life."

After all, there are degrees of happiness, just as there are degrees to all of your emotions— grief, anger, greed, contentment, etc. Name the emotion and there's likely a degree of it present. I've known plenty of folks who appear to be happy doing something other than working on leaving a legacy or learning a new skill. Sure, those people may be happy, but are they as happy as they could be if they were working on leaving a legacy? Which spawns the question: Are they *truly* happy?

Maybe they're a five or a six on the happiness scale, but a five or a six is not good enough for me. I'm shooting for a ten.

Here's my favorite quote from my favorite business book (*Good to Great*) by my all-time favorite business author, Jim Collins. In the course of discussing what it takes to turn a good business into a great business, he gets downright personal with the following statement:

> *"For in the end, it is impossible to have a great life unless it is a meaningful life. And it is very difficult to have a meaningful life without meaningful work."*

As stated earlier, I see no reason why meaningful work should end just because we reach a specified age or achieve a specified goal. If we still have the capacity to do meaningful work, then we should continue doing it. In addition to all of the benefits derived from pursuing a meaningful life, keeping busy pursuing meaningful work is the best anti-aging remedy around.

One can't start doing that meaningful work without making a transition, which will include taking a new direction and adopting a new role in life. The following chapter will provide a starting point for making that transition.

Chapter Six

When the Day Job Ends, A New Life Begins

"Don't simply retire from something; have something to retire to."
— Harry Emerson Fosdick

In April of 1990, feeling a sense of freedom on the one hand and an impending vacuum on the other, I closed the door to my office and walked out of the business I'd founded 18 long years prior, never to return. I had been meeting payrolls (sometimes just barely) for all of those years and, at last count, had 200 employees. Managing that large number of people was outside of my comfort zone. I was 54 years old at the time and was sure there must be something different for me to be doing——something new, something exciting, something that didn't involve the managing and motivating of people.

"How exciting this new life of mine is going to be," I can remember thinking. Mary and I would have no responsibilities outside ourselves. We were moving from Minnesota, the land of eternal winters, to California, the land of eternal summers. How sweet it would be with nothing but sun, surf, and golf

365 days a year. Every day would be a holiday. Life doesn't get much better than that.

It didn't take long to learn that life *can* be much better than that. For me, holidays had always been fun because they had a beginning and an end, but without that beginning and end holidays get old, just like any other period of time that doesn't include a goal with a purpose to reach. A month after arriving in San Diego, after 30 consecutive days of sun, surf, and golf, I was ready for something new. Something stimulating. This new life of never-ending holidays wasn't going to work for me.

I'm not saying everyone is going to have a problem with endless holidays, but I did. In truth, I found myself missing elements of my business. I missed many of my employees, I missed the excitement of the chase, I missed the adrenaline rush that comes from creating a plan and then meeting or exceeding it. I missed not having a purpose, a goal, or a reason to get excited about the upcoming day.

I should have realized that this was going to happen. Looking back, I should have developed a plan for this new stage of life. Had I done that, I would have realized that this retirement-testing step was only the beginning step of a process to determine what the rest of my life would look like. Had I developed a plan, I would have been aware that flunking retirement was OK, that it was a necessary part of charting my path. I would have known that there were four other key steps that lay ahead.

The Four Steps to Determine What Happens Next

Step #1: Retirement. Give it a try, and make every day a Saturday. Play golf, go fishing, mow the yard, take a nap, balance the checkbook, start a new novel, watch TV, fix what's broken, go shopping, check out the Weather Channel, read the newspaper, head for Starbucks, go to a movie, meet the new neighbors down the street. If you can enjoy activities like this— week after week, month after month, year after year- -then go no further, stop right here. It looks like retirement is right up your alley.

Step #2: Start a new hobby or immerse yourself in an old one. Take up a creative art like painting, writing, sculpting, ceramics, or crocheting, the list goes on. Try something new. Learn a software program, play bridge, take music lessons, go bird-watching, check out Ancestry.com—there's no end to the hobbies you can pursue. A new hobby can stimulate you, yet leave you with plenty of time to mow the yard or wash the car or get out of town. Who knows, that new hobby might turn into something unique and exciting—a business, perhaps, or a nonprofit. Or it may simply be enjoyable enough that you don't need to move on to step #3.

Step #3: Find something from your background that interests you and turn it into part-time work. Love golf? Look for starter positions at your local golf courses. Love teaching? Find a local organization that needs instructors with your skills. Love writing? Try blogging or writing a CoolREADS book if you're an expert on something. If you enjoy painting, woodworking, sculpting, or any of the hobby categories that evolve from step #2, try building an inventory of your handiwork and then work a weekend art show.

Step #4: Start an encore career. If the first three steps didn't work, maybe, like me, you're ready to start an encore career. Remember what it was like when you first started your working career? It was scary, but you enjoyed meeting new people and learning new skills—every day was a learning experience. But this time, the pressure will not be the same as it was 30-some years ago. This time, if you fail, you'll still know where your next meal is coming from. Sure, failure will sting, but in this case it's nothing more than an inconvenience and a relatively minor one at that. If what you did didn't work, stop, regroup, and start all over again.

I'll admit that I have a slight bias against retirement. (Maybe more than slight?) There are a number of reasons why this is the case, most of which I've talked about earlier. But there is one more reason that, for people like me, eschewing retirement and moving on to steps two, three, and especially four are the only viable options after we've finished our day job career. To explain this bias of mine, put yourself in my shoes in the following scenario that took place years ago:

It's a sunny and warm mid-April day. Winter is a fading memory, except for the dirty piles of snow left over from a late-spring snowfall. Driving through one of our local retirement communities, I glance out the window and spot a homeowner, a man approximately my age, raking snow on his lawn. Yes, raking snow. On his lawn. It seems a pile of the white stuff alongside his driveway had survived the warm weather, and he was raking it, spreading it out, hoping (I assume) to hasten the melting process.

The image of this man on a sunny spring day, when there were a million constructive things to do, raking snow on his lawn has been frozen in my mind for the ten years or so since I stumbled on the scene. I can't shake that vision or the implication behind it. Did the man have nothing better to do with his time than rake snow? What's his next big event of the day—paying bills? Waiting for the postman? Sorry, but that kind of a life would never work for me. While I assume that man would have answered the "Are you enjoying retirement?" questionnaire with "Yes, I'm quite happy," I want no part of his kind of happy.

For those of you who want something more out of life than raking snow, feel free to give step one a try anyway, just for fun, even though you know that an encore career will probably be your final step.

Assuming you've arrived at step four and that an encore career is your choice, the following two chapters will provide you with options on how to spend this new and exciting gap period of your life.

Chapter Seven

Encore Option #1:
Follow a Path That Already Exists

"I often think about dogs when I think about work and retirement. There are many breeds of dogs that just need to be working, and useful, or have a job of some kind, in order to be happy. Otherwise they are neurotically barking, scratching, or tearing up the sofa. A working dog needs to work. And I am a working dog."

— Martha Sherrill

This movement to alter the retirement landscape is nothing new; the revolution has been gathering steam for years. As a result, a number of organizations have been created to provide definitive options for those of us who have no interest in retiring. There are organizations in the following list for everyone; for people who want to broaden their knowledge, or meet like-minded people, or who simply want to find meaningful work or volunteer experiences.

Organizations Offering Advice and Direction

Encore.org is a nonprofit dedicated to promoting "second acts for the greater good" for those over 50. Encore.org.

Community colleges offer a wide variety of encore career courses, especially in such fields as healthcare, social services, and teaching.

Life Planning Network is a community of professionals and organizations from diverse disciplines dedicated to helping people navigate the second half of their life. Lifeplanningnetwork.org.

Life Reimagined is an AARP program designed to help people over 50 navigate life's changes and challenges. Lifereimagined.aarp.org.

RetiredBrains helps baby boomers, retirees, and those planning their retirement to be happy, healthy, and prosperous. RetiredBrains.com.

The American Academy of Anti-Aging Medicine spreads awareness about innovative, cutting-edge science and research for those considering encore careers, in addition to sharing treatment modalities designed to prolong the human life span. A4m.com.

Work Reimagined is a partnership between AARP and LinkedIn that offers a social community for people with more than 25 years of work experience. Workreimagined.org.

Organizations Offering Opportunities to Get Involved

Civic Ventures is a California-based nonprofit think tank and incubator for social entrepreneurship. Civic Ventures includes two main themes: (1) second careers with meaning and (2) social entrepreneurship. Their tag line is an enticing "second acts for the greater good." Encore.org.

Encore Fellowship matches seasoned professionals with social purpose organizations in high-impact, paid, and transitional assignments. Encore.org/fellowships.

National Service Organizations are government-supported service programs, some of which you've probably heard of (Peace Corps and AmeriCorps) and some of which you probably haven't (Senior Corps and Oasis Lifelong Adventure). Senior Corps (seniorcorps.gov) and Oasis Lifelong Adventure (oasisnet.org) offer opportunities exclusively for people over 55.

Etsy is an online marketplace for a wide variety of homemade, creative products, offering its members the opportunity to turn arts, crafts, and hobbies into businesses. Etsy.com.

Pivot Planet connects their expert advisors with people around the world who are looking to "pivot" from an existing career to a new career or to enhance their current job skills. PivotPlanet.com.

PrimeCB.com connects experienced and retired workers with potential employers. PrimeCB.com.

ReServe is a New York-based social impact organization for people over 55. ReServe matches the talent of people over 55 with social service and government organizations that can use their expertise. ReServeinc.org.

RetirementJobs.com offers job search services for people over 50. Retirementjobs.com.

SCORE (Service Corp of Retired Executives) is a national volunteer-based organization of retired business people that helps small-business owners solve their business problems. SCORE.org.

Workforce 50 offers job and educational opportunities for boomers, seniors, and experienced workers over 50. Workforce50.com.

YourEncore.com is an online search site that matches retired scientists and engineers with employers. Yourencore.com.

Organizations Offering Volunteer Opportunities

Volunteer Match includes a data base of over 100,000 nonprofits around the world that need help. Volunteermatch.org.

Serve.Gov is a federally sponsored search portal charged with promoting and fostering volunteering and national service in America. Serve.gov.

Allforgood.org is a site offering nonprofits around the U.S. the chance to post their volunteering opportunities online. Allforgood.org.

Create the Good is an AARP-sponsored site offering notifications of new opportunities to volunteer in your area. Createthegood.org.

Idealist offers a listing of volunteer opportunities, internships, and jobs around the world. Idealist.org.

HandsOn Network is a Points of Light subsidiary that includes a network of 250 volunteer centers connecting people with volunteer opportunities. Handsonnetwork.org.

Catchafire offers nonprofits the opportunity to connect with passionate, pro bono professionals looking to donate their skills. Catchafire.org.

Organizations Offering Opportunities to Women

The Transition Network is an inclusive community of professional women, aged 50 and forward, whose changing life situations lead them to seek new connections, resources, and opportunities. Thetransitionnetwork.org.

Vibrant Nation is an online community for women over 50. VibrantNation.com.

Women for Hire is an online resource offering ideas, resources, and advice for women wanting to work at home. Womenforhire.com.

Today, more than ever, this nation of ours loves to assemble organizations designed to bring its citizens together—to solve problems, create opportunities, or make their voices heard. Every U.S. community of any size has a Chamber of Commerce, a Rotary, a VFW, and a League of Women Voters, not to mention a large collection of nonprofits. There are opportunities for everyone.

For those of you who aren't "joiners" of organizations, and the U.S. is chock-full of those people too, there are as many opportunities to follow a path less traveled as there are to join something already in existence. The following chapter is written for you.

Chapter Eight

Encore Option #2: Create Your Own Path

"Michelangelo was carving the Rondanini Pietà just before he died at age 89, Verdi finished his opera 'Falstaff' at age 80, Andy Rooney died at age 92 (one month after his final 60 Minutes broadcast), Morley Safer passed away at age 85 (eight days after he retired), and Jimmy Carter is still making things happen at age 92."

— Jim Schell

Some people prefer not to reinvent the wheel. Others intend either to change it or downright replace it. The preceding chapter was written for those people who are satisfied to use the wheel as it presently exists. This chapter is for the reinventors, the changers, and the disrupters, for those people who prefer to do things their way.

I'm going to use my own encore careers as a template to help you figure out how you can navigate what can be a hugely exciting phase of your life. In order to understand how my encore careers came to pass, it is first necessary to remind you of a few personal facts.

As shared earlier, my working career was as an entrepreneur. Today I'm a poster child for career reinvention and am currently in the midst of my third encore career. Those three careers include: (1) writer, (2) social entrepreneur, and (3) a hybrid of my three previous careers (entrepreneur, writer, and social entrepreneur).

I am, at the core, a card-carrying entrepreneur, which means my DNA includes most of the textbook strengths and weaknesses that the typical entrepreneur shares. If you promise not to tell, I'll share three of my most glaring character weaknesses with you that, paradoxically, led me down the entrepreneurial path and into my three encore careers.

Those three character weaknesses are:

1. **Short attention span.** I have difficulty focusing on tasks or projects for long periods of time. As a result, I want to get things done quickly, allowing me to move on to whatever is next. ("Variety," as my mother used to say, "is the spice of life.")

2. **Trouble following instructions.** For whatever misguided reason, I seem to think that I have more important things to do than read instructions or listen to directions, which means I'm likely to skip them entirely and dive headfirst into whatever the project is. More often than not, this leads to misdirection. (But it sure helps in getting shit done, sooner rather than later.)

3. **Things done MY way.** Yes, I'll listen, but I need to have the last word. (This is not always the case at home, I should add.)

Do any of these three entrepreneurial-based weaknesses apply to you? (Or, God forbid, all three?) If so, this chapter is right up your alley. Hopefully, what will also be right up your alley is a spark of an idea on how you can create and develop at least one encore career of your own.

I more or less drifted (or was it stumbled?) into my three encore careers. After considering several encore career alternatives (starting a new business, consulting, working for a nonprofit), I shrugged my shoulders and decided to dive into step three from chapter six (find something from your background that interests you and turn it into part-time work), which led to encore career #1——turning my writing hobby into a career. Following is a description of that career along with the lessons learned.

Encore Career #1

Since I'd been a voracious reader since childhood, I figured I'd try writing. Specifically, I'd set a goal to become a published author. In eight years I published six nonfiction books: four by New York houses and two self-published. I also wrote several bombs—fiction and nonfiction—that never saw the light of day, while in-between penning dozens of forgettable magazine articles. Fortunately, there were no such things as blogs back in those pre-Internet days or I'm sure I would have given that a try too.

Yes, I made a token amount of money from encore career #1, but not enough to pay the heating bills, let alone take fancy vacations. Writing, similar to many creative-type endeavors, only pays well for the upper five percent of its participants. For the rest of us it is a labor of love. However, I did come to understand the business of writing, from publishing to marketing to distribution. These lessons, serendipitously, would lead almost three decades later to me starting Lights On Publishing, the business that published this CoolREADS book. (Never discount the value of learning something new. Sooner or later it may come back to roost.)

The lesson learned from encore career #1 is to follow those four steps outlined in chapter six. Writing (and reading) had been part of my life since I was old enough to read Hemingway and Jack London, thus it was a perfect segue for turning a hobby into a business. For many years, hardly a day went by when I didn't log at least a few hundred words. I originally started writing with no great financial aspirations, but once my first book was published, I adopted it as a full-fledged career.

Who knows, there may be a future for you hidden somewhere in the throes of the various hobbies and interests that have dotted your life. Dive deeply into them and study their nuances. Is there by chance a viable career opportunity imbedded within one of them? If that opportunity is not in the creative part, then maybe you'll find it in the back-end (the organizational, distribution, administrative, and/or marketing part).

There are a wide range of ways to learn about the inner workings of a prospective career. Take a class at your local community college or university, network with someone who already works in that career field, read books on the topic, consult your favorite search engine, follow blogs, and utilize social media. There is a variety of offline and online information available to help you do the research.

Assuming you come up with an idea for your own encore career #1, set a goal for yourself before you dive in. Not a goal to make money, mind you, but rather to learn about both the creative and business-related aspects of the career. (The goal should include a timeline; i.e., when you intend to start and finish the various elements of your goal.) In the writing world, for instance, in addition to learning how to ratchet up your writing skills, you should also learn about business-related topics, such as agents, publishing (both institutional and self-publishing), marketing, and distribution. Every creative career has an infrastructure lurking behind it. Study that infrastructure and discover the opportunities within that niche that might be adaptable to your skills. Who knows, there could be an encore career nestled somewhere within it.

I suggest that you don't set any financial goals for yourself at the outset; those can come later (if the niche you've chosen is right and you're the right person for it). The worst thing that can result from trying something new is that you'll learn something about a career field that interests you and then move on. The best thing would be that you figure out how to monetize your idea and create a full-fledged encore career.

The search for subsequent careers, incidentally, assumes that you need to generate income from whatever it is you choose to do. If income generation is not a priority, then the search becomes much easier. Omit the monetization requirement and your landscape of opportunities expands. A volunteer-based encore career has more options to pursue than a career that requires a financial return.

Encore Career #2

In keeping with my attention-span-shortage issue, six years after starting what had become a semi-successful writing career, encore career #2 raised its opportunistic head. We had moved to Bend, Oregon, in 1994, the harried culture of Southern California proving to be too much for two Midwesterners. In 1996, while still engrossed in a personally rewarding but lonely writing career, I decided I needed an adrenaline recharge. This meant I needed to get involved with the kind of people that recharge me: other entrepreneurs.

With that objective in mind, I started a nonprofit in Bend called Opportunity Knocks (OK), which assembles peer-to-peer teams of entrepreneurs, thereby creating an advisory board environment for them to solve each other's problems. Not only does OK include current entrepreneurs as its members, it also includes past ones who serve as facilitators for its teams. In a few short years Opportunity Knocks grew to include several hundred current entrepreneurs along with four dozen ex-entrepreneurs (aka volunteer facilitators) and became a full-scale nonprofit 501(c)(6) with an annual budget in excess of $100,000. We hired an executive director to lead the organization while a board of directors provided the vision and strategic direction.

Several years later a turnaround opportunity presented itself at our local Humane Society. Three years of sometimes unpleasant but eventually rewarding work there resulted in a well-oiled organization with a brand-spanking-new $2.1 million shelter. As a result of my experiences with OK and the Humane Society, by 2003 I was hooked on the nonprofit world and its mission of social impact. I not only discovered an encore career where I could learn new skills, it was also rife with opportunities to leave a legacy. In the following ten years I would lead turnarounds at two more nonprofits and start five new ones. (Incidentally, the lessons I learned during those years also led to the writing of another book in the CoolREADS series: *How to Recharge Your Nonprofit: Introducing the Entrepreneurial Team Board of Directors*.)

What lesson did I learn from encore career #2? If you're looking to make a difference and be personally fulfilled at the same time, the nonprofit sector is full of juicy opportunities. For those of you with an entrepreneurial bent, you can do as I did——create an encore career by fixing struggling nonprofits (there will be no shortage of opportunities) or start new ones.

I should mention that there is a designation for people who work in the nonprofit sphere (usually as executive directors or board chairs) and who manage and oversee their organizations with an entrepreneurial bent. That designation is "social entrepreneur," which can be defined as "someone who utilizes entrepreneurial visions and principals to create, manage, and oversee a venture designed to make social change." A social entrepreneur is to the nonprofit world what an entrepreneur is to the for-profit sector (except that the for-profit entrepreneur has a single bottom line, to do well, while the social entrepreneur has a double bottom line, to do well *and* to do good). In recent years the principles that drive for-profit entrepreneurs have become an integral part of the social entrepreneur's tool kit. As a result, the nonprofit world has become much more vibrant, exciting, and receptive to change.

For those encore career seekers who possess managerial skills, the board of director model that drives the nonprofit world provides fertile grounds for involvement. Sadly, most nonprofit boards consist largely of people who care about the mission but don't have the business skills and background required to run a successful organization. The key to creating or working with a successful nonprofit is to start with a vibrant board of directors. Vibrant boards are developed by combining sound board-recruiting practices with professional leadership, two skills that people with management backgrounds typically possess. Once a vibrant board is assembled and in good working order, a contributing and functioning organization is sure to follow.

My community of Bend, Oregon (population 90,000), has somewhere between 100 and 150 functional nonprofits at work in various social service and recreational niches. Around 20 percent of those nonprofits can be categorized as excellent, while the other 80 percent range from mediocre to dysfunctional. The leadership and management guidance that that 80 percent will need to up their game will typically come from people with business backgrounds. Thus, board members with finance, marketing, organizational, or administrative skills are always needed for successful boards. If these skills are part of your arsenal, there is a huge opportunity to make an impact in the nonprofit world. A little research should turn up plenty of local organizations in need of your assistance.

So, how might you undertake that "little research"? Communities of every size have a nonprofit-related network that includes one or more consultants who make their living helping nonprofits solve their problems. (My community has four.) By interviewing local nonprofit executive directors, you can find out who those nonprofit consultants are. Once located, get an audience with one or more of them; they can advise you on which nonprofits are in need of a board restructure or a new executive director or a better business model. Ask enough questions and you'll learn where the opportunities lie for someone with your skills. Good board members do not grow on trees, so once you've identified a nonprofit or two that you'd be interested in helping, contact the board chair and interview him or her—most of them will happily welcome an inquiry from someone who has the required skills and is motivated to help his or her nonprofit succeed.

Occasionally a volunteer experience has the potential to turn into a salaried opportunity. For four years I was the for-hire executive director of a poverty reduction nonprofit in desperate need of a turnaround. Yes, I was compensated for my services. It was the first employee-type job I had had in 35 years. The organization hired me because of my past experience with rejiggering organizations. Such remuneration-based opportunities are few and far between, so if compensation is a necessary element of your encore career, opportunities in the nonprofit world typically will not evolve from a volunteer beginning. Most paid positions within the nonprofit sector are filled as a result of organized job searches for qualified applicants.

Encore Career #3

Today I'm happily immersed in encore career #3, which is a hybrid of my first working career (entrepreneur) and the two previous encore careers (writer and social entrepreneur). As you will see from the bullet points below, encore career #3 includes a wide range of activities, most of which borrowed from my previous day-job and encore careers. I intentionally initiated this career knowing that over the years I had developed a number of new skills from both the for-profit and nonprofit sectors. When combined, I became one of the few people in my community armed to work across the nonprofit and for-profit sectors. There is a wide range of opportunities in every community for someone who is able to work in multiple sectors.

Following is a list of some of the activities I'm currently involved in with encore career #3 and how they interrelate with previous careers. As you review this list, think of ways you can mix and match the skills you've garnered from your previous experiences with ideas you have for your first, or subsequent, encore career. Presently (or recently), I:

- Serve on two for-profit boards: I bring to the boards business skills from my working (pre-encore) entrepreneurial career.
- Serve on three non-profit boards: I bring to the boards entrepreneurial skills from my working career and

nonprofit skills from my social entrepreneur encore career #2.

- Founded a for-profit publishing business: I bring to the business my entrepreneurial skills from my working career and my knowledge of the publishing industry from encore career #1.
- Authored six CoolREADS on entrepreneurship and nonprofits: I bring to the business my writing skills from encore career #2.
- Formally mentor four young people (and informally many more): I bring to the mentoring experience the skills learned from one working career and three encore careers.
- Actively work to make my community a better place to live: I bring to the table the skills I learned from all four careers.

Getting to the stage of life where you can contribute to a wide variety of local causes takes years of experience. For me, the accumulation of the encore skills I needed began somewhere around age 55. Today, I've had 25 years to learn the skills I needed and then apply those lessons to the betterment of my community. That's 25 years of learning and doing. It wasn't always easy, and it wasn't always fun, but it was all part of the encore evolution.

Each year of those 25 has been valuable. I've worked with a lot of committed and passionate people. Together we've left a trail of legacies that have benefited our community and fulfilled my need to be working on the personal legacy Stephen Covey wrote about.

Chapter Nine

Making the Transition

"Sooner or later I'm going to die, but I'm never going to retire."
— Margaret Mead

Can you imagine what the first day of your non-working life is going to be like? Have you thought about that day at all? What time you'll get up in the morning, what you'll have for breakfast, what you'll do for the rest of the day? Who will you talk to? What will you think about as you're munching your toast and sipping your coffee?

Let me venture a guess as to what you *won't* be thinking about. You won't be thinking about whether or not you need a new coffee maker. Or which program you should watch on TV. Or what you are going to do for lunch, or dinner, or what time you will be going to bed.

Rather, you'll be thinking about whether or not this will be a typical day in your life from this point forward. If it won't, how will it be different? Will you need a project to pursue? Will you need a goal to achieve? Now that you aren't around a host of co-workers all day, who will you spend your time with? Doing what? What will be transferable from your old life to your new life? What won't? In short, the details of the day won't be on your mind. The direction of your life will be what consumes your thoughts.

I'm not saying you'll need to answer all of those directional questions on that first morning of your new life. You've assumedly thought about many of them before, especially those related to your financial needs. On that very first morning you'll probably be thinking about the macro and strategic elements of your life, not the day-to-day stuff.

Here are five suggestions of the kind of specific macro and strategic topics you should be noodling on that very first morning:

- **Your timeline:** If you aren't sure what will make you want to get up in the morning, don't rush the decision. The rest of your life is (hopefully) going to last a long time. Any decisions you make today will have long-term implications tomorrow.
- **Your health:** Most experts are quick to lecture that the degree to which you enjoy your retirement (or un-retirement) will depend largely upon your health. What are you going to do to ensure that you stay healthy? When are you going to start? How much time are you going to commit to maintaining and improving your health? Should you get off on the right foot and begin

this morning? Don't procrastinate on this one; the sooner you get started the better.

- **Stephen Covey's four Ls:** Which of the four Ls (live, love, learn, and leave a legacy) will you require in order to make yourself happy? What are you going to do to ensure that all four of them are in sync?

- **Success:** How will you define success in your post-working life? You once knew exactly what success looked like: an increase in pay, more vacation time, or a key project consummated. Once defined, the pursuit of success in your post-working career years will provide you with a direction to follow and a goal to pursue.

- **Things to watch out for:**

  TV: TV is the world's greatest time suck and the enemy of free thinking. Aging has enough unavoidable downsides as it is without adding a slew of needless activities to your daily routine. An hour or so of TV in a day is passable, any more than that is a waste of your time.

  Alcohol: I've seen too many lives negatively impacted by the side effects of too much alcohol. You've surely seen plenty of them too. Don't let three o'clock become the new five o'clock.

  Curmudgeon-ism: Listen, ask questions, hear both sides, and don't be a naysayer. There is plenty to learn and to feel good about. Be positive and interesting. No one wants to listen to your tales of woe.

Fuddy-duddy-ism: There's more to talk about than your health, your pets, and your grandchildren. Stay informed. Be relevant. Be interesting.

Balance: Whatever you decide to focus on in your new life, be sure to maintain a healthy balance. Keep all of your work, play, travel, and family bases covered.

I didn't include finances in this list because you've no doubt been thinking about (and hopefully working on) that topic for years. There is an abundance of books and web-based information available on the topic of managing your financial life after your working days are finished. This CoolREADS is not one of those, but I'm a relentless advocate of getting your financial life in order, both pre- and post-retirement. If you haven't done this already, you're starting off on the wrong foot.

Nolan Bushnell, the ageless founder of Atari, famously said that "anyone who can take a shower can have a good idea; what matters is what happens after you towel off." It's one of my favorite business and life adages because it reminds me that whatever we do will be little more than a good idea unless we execute it. Bushnell realized that idea generation is the easy part. The execution is the tough part and is solely up to us.

Chapter Ten

Support Matters

I'm hoping that this CoolREADS has impacted your thinking on retirement and that you will, when the time comes, choose to follow a path designed to keep your mind active, your spirit involved, and your intentions focused on doing something Jim Collins would identify as meaningful.

But first, before you set out to do all that, there are two factors that must be considered before you begin pursuing an encore career, especially if that career includes volunteering a significant amount of your time without being compensated. The first of those two factors is—yes, you guessed it— MONEY.

Money matters for everyone. Fortunately, our family had enough of it to allow me the freedom to spend my time doing whatever I saw fit. If your financial situation doesn't allow you to do what I did, you may need to supplement your retirement savings in order to make ends meet. This need to generate income shouldn't, however, preclude you from giving back, but it could limit the amount of time you can allot to doing meaningful volunteer work. A couple of hours of financial math should help you make that determination.

Unless you're a Fortune 500 CEO, a professional athlete, or your surname is Rockefeller, Social Security alone will not be enough to assure a comfortable retirement. Following is a list of potential revenue-generating opportunities:

Income Options After Your Day Job is Finished

Social Security: You've already paid in an amount equal to the first dozen-or-so years of retirement through your Social Security deductions. Any years past that number will be a bonus, and the federal government will pick up the tab. (Or, more specifically, by tomorrow's contributors to the Social Security system). Current estimates predict that Social Security will have enough assets to continue paying out through 2034. However, there are no guarantees after that. Elect the right politicians and (hopefully) they will do something to resolve the threat of this approaching deadline.

401(k)s and IRAs: If you're not a government employee and have spent your career within the private sector, hopefully you worked for an employer who offered a employer match for a company-sponsored 401(k) plan. Also, (again, hopefully) you took maximum advantage of any opportunities to make your own contributions to the plan.

Pensions: If you're a government employee or one of the very few (and extremely fortunate) private-sector retirees who still receive pensions, this will likely be your primary source of retirement. Many people initially determine who they are going to work for depending upon the retirement options the employer offers. Unfortunately, there aren't many private-sector employers today that offer pension opportunities. If late-life security is a worry that keeps you up at night, I suggest you take a hard look at government employment.

Part-time Work: There are many helpful venues for finding part-time work. Check Craigslist or your local job-search website and let your fingers do the rest. Also, opportunities for part-time work may include consulting gigs within your area of expertise.

Home Equity: There are two ways to tap into your home equity: (1) downsize your current residence to a less expensive house and/or (2) utilize a reverse mortgage. Consult a local real estate professional for advice on how to navigate reverse mortgages.

Real Estate: Retirees who are handy around the

house and have DIY skills can either buy and maintain rental property or rent out parts of their homes (lofts, garages, basements).

Stocks, Bonds, Annuities, and Other Investments: This has always been my favorite retirement vehicle, although not necessarily my number one income contributor. I invest for the long term and try not to worry about the inevitable downturns (although, admittedly, 2008 tested that resolve).

Savings Accounts and Certificates of Deposit: As this is written, interest rates on these two options are abysmal, but some people still use them as they are the gold standard of liquidity.

Investing in Small Businesses: Since entrepreneurship was my career of choice, I have, over my post-day-job years, made a number of investments in startup small businesses. A note to those of you who are considering this route: Be sure to invest in the people who are running the business, not in whatever it is that the business does.

Inheritance: Ah, don't we all wish that this were an option. However, for some fortunate gene-pool folks, inheritance can play a major role in their retirement plans.

As suggested earlier, there is plenty of information available online to help you make the key financial decisions necessary to enjoy this time of your life. Pursuit of the financial resources needed for a comfortable late-life lifestyle should always be at the top of your to-do list.

The second factor to consider before diving into an encore career is support. More specifically, the backing and encouragement received from your spouse, partner, or family. Such support will be more likely to happen if you have your financial ducks in a line.

I've been on the receiving end of the kind of support I'm talking about. Since age 55, I've spent the majority of my weekdays donating time and energy to make my community a better place to live. I maintain a daily schedule of formal and informal meetings and coffee shop interactions (which is not unlike when I managed my own businesses). However, at the end of the day, in lieu of money, I'm compensated by the feelings of accomplishment that come from the work that I do.

Meanwhile, for the past 30 years Mary, who is the owner of a small business, heads to work in the morning at the same time I do. However, she has the responsibilities of managing employees, meeting deadlines, and serving customers. If something isn't fun, she does it anyway. For that she gets paid, which means she contributes to our family's well-being.

Meanwhile, I contribute very little these days, other than some interesting dinnertime conversations. However, I add to our monthly expenses, spending on such things as gas, food, and entertainment. I end most of my days on a high while Mary ends many of hers with a headache.

She is proud of our family's contribution to the greater good, even though hers is more passive than mine. She gives me the latitude to do whatever I want to do in a volunteer vein, even though the lawn might need mowing at the time. Without her support, there would be no encore career for me.

This chapter is for those of you who intend to spend a significant amount of your encore-career making the world a better place in the way I've described. To your friends and the people you work with, such a career choice may appear to be the best of all possible worlds. Not only is giving back good for the soul, it is usually fun. But before you make that choice, before you make an obligation that will financially and emotionally impact those you love, they need to sign on to your commitment.

You can encourage that support by making sure your family's financial needs are met. Once you've done that, the support is sure to come.

Chapter Eleven

Tips and Suggestions

There is much to learn about remaining active, staying relevant, and getting involved throughout the aging process. Given the breadth and complexity of the process, following are a number of tips and suggestions that don't have a home in this book.

- **Be interested and interesting.** "Interested is interesting" was my mother's favorite adage, and it's still as relevant today as it was 40 years ago. If you want to be relevant and vibrant as you get older, learn to ask questions. Lots of questions. Older people who ask questions are more interested in learning than they are in talking about themselves.

- **Be passionate about whatever you decide to do.** One of the favorite principles of business is "passion sells." This principle affirms that if you want to sell something—to your customers, your bankers, or your employees—it's your passion that will create the relationships you need to be effective. This principle applies to all senior citizens, whether they choose to pursue an encore career or not. The more passionate you are about life and your role in it, the more likely it will be that active and interesting people will want to be associated with you.

- **Stay local.** These days, it's easy to be frustrated by your local, state, or federal governments, but don't be a geezer and sit around your local coffee shop complaining about all the things wrong with the world. There are plenty of opportunities in your neighborhood or in your community to do something about whatever is wrong. You can't always impact what goes on in Washington, D.C. or your state capitol, but you *can* impact what happens in your own hometown.

- **Get involved.** Find ways to meet new people and connect within your community. You don't need to join your local Rotary or the Chamber of Commerce (although those are options), but you can get involved in projects that interest you. It's no different than it was when you were in school; it's the company you keep that will most impact your life.

- **Get wired.** If an encore career is in your future, don't allow technology to leave you in the dust. Whatever you end up pursuing, you can bet that technology will be a part of it. You don't have to try and keep up with technology—you'd die trying—but you can't ignore it either.

- **Upgrade your email.** Make sure your email address is professional, up to date, and uses your name (for example, jim.schell5@gmail.com).

- **Expand your online network.** Become familiar with LinkedIn and Facebook. Take the time to professionalize your LinkedIn page and keep it up to date. Include a picture and a well-written, enticing Introduction.

- **Consider a coach.** There are coaches whose niche is to help people transition to encore careers. Check out coachfederation.org.

- **Get educated.** For those of you who want to go back to school, Laura Gilbert has written a book just for you: *Back to School for Grownups.* UCLA Extension offers courses providing baby boomers with marketable skills for careers in such fields as nonprofit management, counseling, and environmental sustainability.

- **Volunteer for a nonprofit board.** Before you do, learn how to become a contributing board of director's member. Check out bridgestar.org, boardsource.org, or boardnetusa.org. Also, check out our CoolREADS entitled *How to Recharge Your Nonprofit: Introducing the Entrepreneurial Team Board of Directors.*

Conclusion

"Choose a work that you love and you won't have to work another day." – **Confucius**

The concept of giving back in our later years is nothing new. The ancient Greeks figured it out thousands of years before we did. An anonymous proverb proclaims: "Society grows great when old men plant trees whose shade they know they shall never sit in." It paints a picture for future generations of the legacy that comes from leaving behind something meaningful--a tree, a healthy nonprofit, or a life changed. Those old men who were planting trees were dedicated to leaving the world just a little bit better than they found it. One can only imagine what would happen if all of the world's old men and women planted a tree before they said goodbye: Patagonia could focus its resources elsewhere, the Amazon basin could breathe easier again, and Greenpeace could get rid of all their ships.

The fascinating thing about giving back is that not only is it altruism at work, there is also a touch of selfishness involved. Studies have shown that people who give back, not only in their post-retirement years but also in their working careers, gain significantly from the experience. Those gains include improvements in mental health, a feeling of productivity, and a pronounced increase in social activity.

I recently read a blog post by T. Boone Pickens, an American business magnate and financier. In his post, Boone quotes a friend of his who made the following comment: "Boone has been in the prime of his life three times." When I read that comment I felt a rush of elation, a sense of bonding. I know exactly of what Boone's friend speaks.

For some of us, and I hope you're included, one "prime" is not enough.

Author's Note

In the world of nonfiction literature there are two kinds of books, Big Fat Books and Little Skinny CoolREADS. While the Big Fat Books (BFBs) are longer reads and sell for $25 instead of $10, there are times when they're worth the additional money and the three hours it takes to read them. So it is with *The Big Shift*, Marc Freedman's BFB that was an eye-opener for me when I read it a number of years ago. Before I read *The Big Shift*, I considered myself an outlier in the world of people over 65—pursuing—and loving—my occasionally stressful, always meaningful version of un-retirement. "What's wrong with me?" I remember thinking. My friends are playing golf on weekday afternoons while I'm sitting in a coffee shop listening to someone's problem.

Thank you, Marc Freedman, for opening my eyes to the fact that there are millions of people like me out there keeping their heads down, grinding away, and helping the world solve its never-ending problems. If the message in this CoolREADS resonates with you and you want to dive deeper into the topic of encore careers, purchase Marc Freedman's book.

And then go have fun!

Made in the USA
Middletown, DE
13 September 2023

38463508R00044